WINTERSLOW C.E. AIDED SCHOOL
WILTSHIRE

Special Occasions

GRAHAM OWEN and ALISON SEAMAN

WAYLAND

Festivals
Jesus and Mary
Special Occasions
Worship

Editor: Carron Brown
Series consultant: Alison Seaman
Designer and typesetter: Jean Wheeler
Cover designer: Steve Wheele Design
Picture researcher: Gina Brown

First published in 1998 by Wayland Publishers Ltd,
61 Western Road, Hove, East Sussex, BN3 1JD

British Library Cataloguing in Publication Data
Seaman, Alison
Special Occasions. – (Looking at Christianity)
1. Rites and ceremonies – Juvenile literature
2. Fasts and feasts – Juvenile literature
I.Title II. Owen, Graham
263.9

ISBN 0 7502 2240 9

Picture acknowledgements
Andes Press Agency/Carlos Reyes-Manzo 7, 10, 11, 12, 13, 17, 18, 19, 25; Church House Publishing 5; Getty Images/Dennis O'Clair 21; Sally and Richard Greenhill 6, 20; David Toase/Redemptionist Publications 14; Christine Osborne 1, 27; Wayland Picture Library 23, /Penny Davies 4, 15, 16, 22, 24, 26, /Angela Hampton 8, 9. Cover photo by Martyn F. Chillmaid.

Printed and bound by EuroGrafica S.p.A., Italy

Contents

Baptism **4**

Special journeys **8**

First communion **12**

Confirmation **14**

Marriage **16**

Remembering **20**

Sunday **24**

Notes for teachers **28**

Glossary **30**

Books to read **31**

Index **32**

All religious words are explained in the glossary.

Baptism

Today is an important day for Scott.

His mum is getting him ready to go to church for his baptism. Everyone has been helping to prepare for this special day.

Lucy's parents have chosen three people to be her godparents.

They will promise to help Lucy as she grows up, to believe and trust in God.

The priest baptises Simon by pouring water over his head.

In the church, everybody stands around the font to watch. Simon is now a member of the whole church family.

A candle is lit for Katie.

Katie's mum is given a baptism candle to take home and keep. When the candle is lit, it will remind all the family of this special day.

# Special journeys

Rawaa is off to the seaside with her friends.

She meets her friends every Sunday at church, but today they are going on their summer outing.

8

This is a day to remember.

Rawaa enjoys being on the beach with her friends from church.

These people are on a special journey called a pilgrimage.

The day of this special journey is one these people will remember. People who travel on a pilgrimage are called pilgrims.

These people are visiting a holy place.

Pilgrims have visited this holy place for hundreds of years. When they come here, they feel close to God.

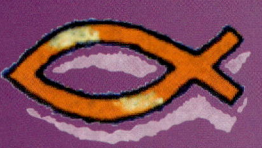# First communion

Sean is being given bread by the priest.

He has been learning about why Christians share bread together.

12

These children have been looking forward to this special day.

They have spent time finding out about their church and what it means to be a Christian. They are glad to have their friends with them to support them.

Confirmation

Jane kneels in front of the bishop.

This is her Confirmation Day. She feels she is now old enough to promise for herself to believe and trust in God.

Ruth is pleased with her new Bible.

It will help her as she learns more about what it means to be a Christian.

Marriage

Duncan and Rachel are getting ready for their wedding day.

They love each other very much and want to spend the rest of their lives together. The priest talks with them about the promises they will make at their marriage service.

Christians remember the last meal Jesus had with his friends.

Jesus told them that he wouldn't be with them for long. When they shared the meal of bread and wine, he told them to remember him whenever they did this together.

Good Friday is the saddest day of the Christian year.

Christians remember that some people turned against Jesus and wanted to kill him. He was put to death on a cross.

These people are helping to carry a cross around their town in Israel.

This is a way for people to remember that Jesus died on a cross. Christians believe he was willing to die for them.

Easter Day

Easter is here. A new day begins.

Christians believe that Jesus came back to life. As they watch the sun rise on Easter Day, they remember that Jesus brings them new life.

Alison and Sam are sharing their Easter eggs on Easter Day.

They cannot decide which one to eat first. Easter eggs remind Christians of Easter when Jesus came back to life.

# Ascension

Christians believe that Jesus is in heaven with his Father.

Christians celebrate this on Ascension Day. Even though they cannot see him they believe he is still with them.

# Pentecost

After Jesus had gone to heaven, his friends did not know what to do.

At Pentecost, Christians remember that God helped Jesus's friends by giving them the gift of the Holy Spirit. This made them brave again and they wanted to go and tell everyone about Jesus.

 Harvest festival

Christians believe that God made the world.

Christians know that God loves and cares for the world. He expects everyone to help look after his wonderful creation.

Michael and Kim have brought Harvest gifts to their church.

Christians give thanks for all of God's gifts on this special day. They bring gifts to say thank you to God for all the good things in life.

Saints' days

Christians remember special people, like Mary the mother of Jesus.

On Saints' Days, Christians say thank you to God for their lives. Some saints are well known, some are not. Since the time of Jesus, all Christians have tried to be like him.

Sunday

Every Sunday is a festival day.

Even though Jesus is no longer alive, Christians believe he is with them when they share bread and wine together.

Notes for teachers

About the pictures

The images used in this series are in many respects as important as the text. The historical nature of the subject requires that we use illustrations and photographs as well as actors' representations to enliven the text for children. The images have been chosen to provide stimuli for discussion and enable children to engage imaginatively with the subject matter.

pp 4–5

The Christian year follows a pattern of festivals that commemorate events in the life of Jesus. Each year, the festivals provide a structure for Christian worship. This book introduces pupils to the major festivals of the Christian calendar and places them into the context of the whole Christian year.

pp 6–7

The preparation for festivals is as important as the festival itself. Advent is a time of preparation for Christmas and starts four Sundays before Christmas Day. Children might be familiar with Advent calendars which normally begin on 1 December. Another popular custom is to construct an Advent ring. This consists of a wreath of evergreen, four coloured candles, one for each Sunday in Advent (colours vary according to tradition), and a central white candle representing Jesus's birth on Christmas Day.

pp 8–9

For Christians, Jesus is understood to be a gift from God. Gifts are exchanged at Christmas to celebrate this event. A central Christian belief is that God, in Jesus, knows what it is to be human. Jesus is usually described as the Son of God. The story of the birth of Jesus is a combination of two Gospel accounts (Matthew and Luke) which give different perspectives on the events. The actual date of Jesus's birth is not known but, since the 4th century, Western Christians have celebrated Jesus's birth on 25 December while Orthodox Christians celebrate it in early January.

pp 10–11

In Luke's Gospel, the birth of Jesus is first announced to shepherds by an angel. The account tells of the shepherds' hasty journey to Bethlehem to see the newborn baby. In Matthew's Gospel, Jesus's family receive important visitors (magi, kings or astrologers) from the East. It describes how they followed a star in order to find Jesus to give him gifts of gold, frankincense and myrrh.

pp 12–13

Traditionally, before the Lent fast begins, rich foods, especially fats, are used up on Shrove Tuesday (from which comes the custom of eating pancakes). In some parts of the world, this festival is known as Mardi Gras (Fat Tuesday) and is marked by elaborate street parades and festivities. The forty days of Lent lead up to Easter. Lent is a time of quiet reflection for Christians, and they may also give up certain foods during this period.

pp 14–15

In some traditions, palm crosses are burnt and the ash used to make the sign of the cross on the forehead of the worshippers. This ashing ceremony is a symbol of forgiveness and a reminder of human mortality. Roughly half-way through Lent there is a break from the austerity of the season with the festival of Mothering Sunday.

pp 16–17

Traditionally on Palm Sunday, palms made into the shape of a cross are blessed and given to worshippers. Palm Sunday is the first day of Holy week, which leads up to the festivals that mark the death and resurrection of Jesus.

Jesus' last week with his disciples, on the eve of his death, is remembered on Maundy Thursday. This significant festival is celebrated in a variety of ways but all remember this Last Supper, when Jesus commanded his disciples to remember him whenever they ate together. This instruction is obeyed when Christians celebrate the Eucharist (also called Mass, Lord's Supper and Holy Communion).

pp 18–19

Jesus was seen as a threat by some of his contemporaries and was subsequently wrongly accused, put on trial and sentenced to death. Crucifixion was the method of capital punishment used at the time by the Roman authorities. The paradox of describing the day as 'Good Friday' comes from Jesus's willingness to die on a cross. This is understood by Christians to be the example of goodness and love for all people. The cross has become the universal symbol for Christians throughout the world.

pp 20–21

The significance of Easter, for Christians, is that after his death on the cross, Jesus is believed to have come back to life after three days. There is a variety of symbols that help Christians understand this complex and difficult belief. On Easter Day, some Christians see the dawn as a powerful reminder of new life. A widespread custom is the exchange of Easter eggs.

pp 22–23

After his resurrection, the New Testament gives accounts of times when Jesus met with his friends and followers. His final parting from them is the event commemorated on Ascension Day. Christians believe that although Jesus is no longer with them, his presence can still be felt in the world. Feelings of loss or separation are ones that could be explored with pupils at this time.

After his Ascension, Jesus' disciples felt a sense of loss and bewilderment. At Pentecost, they experienced a renewed energy to go out and continue the work Jesus had begun. This is known as the 'coming of the Holy Spirit'. The symbols of wind and fire are commonly used to represent the force of the Holy Spirit at work.

pp 24–25

Christians believe they share the responsibility for looking after the world's resources. While Harvest is not part of the Christian calendar, it has become a recognised tradition to give thanks for the fruits of the earth. Harvest thanksgivings are usually held in churches and schools at which prayers of thanks are given for God's creation and gifts are distributed to those who are in need.

pp 26–27

As well as the major festivals, there are individual festival days that commemorate the lives of Christians throughout the ages. As well as famous Christians, all Christians are remembered on All Saints' Day (1 November). Every Sunday is a festival day because it is the day when Jesus rose from the dead. It is traditionally a special day for worship and for many Christians focuses on the sharing of bread and wine at the Eucharist.

Glossary

Advent The preparation time before Christmas.

angel A messenger from God.

Ascension Day Forty days after Easter Day when Jesus went to heaven.

Bible The most important holy book for all Christians.

Christians People who follow the teachings of Jesus Christ.

Christmas The time when Jesus was born.

Easter The time when Jesus was killed and came back to life again.

Good Friday The day when Jesus was killed.

Harvest When Christians say say thank you for God's world.

heaven Christians hope they will go there after they die.

Holy Spirit The presence of God.

Lent The preparation time before Easter.

Pentecost Fifty days after Easter when the disciples received the Holy Spirit.

saints Special people who have followed Jesus's teaching.

Books to read

For children

Bridges to Religions: An Egg for Babcha by Margaret Barratt (Heinemann, 1994)

Festivals of the Christian Year by Lois Rock (Lion, 1996)

My Christian Life by Alison Seaman (Wayland, 1996)

Sunshine Religious Stories: The Story of Easter and The Birth of Jesus by Owen Cole and Judith Lowndes (Heinemann, 1995)

Resources for teachers

CEM Teaching RE Series 5–11 contains publications on all major Christian festivals. Available from CEM, Royal Buildings, Victoria Street, Derby, DE1 1GW

Seasons, Saints and Sticky Tape by Nicola Currie and Jean Thomson (The National Society, 1992)

Shap Calendar of Religious Festivals available from Shap, 36 Causton Street, London, SW1P 4AU

Index

Advent Calendar 6
Advent Ring 7
All Saints' Day 26
Ascension Day 22
Ash Wednesday 14

bread 17, 27

Christmas Day 7, 8
cross 18, 19

Easter Day 20
Easter eggs 21

gifts 8, 11, 25
God 5, 8, 10, 13, 14, 22, 24, 25, 26
Good Friday 18

heaven 22, 23
Holy Spirit 23

Jesus 4, 5, 6, 8, 9, 11, 16, 17, 18, 19, 20, 22, 23, 26, 27

Lent 12, 13, 14, 15

Mary 26
Mothering Sunday 15

Palm Sunday 16

Shrove Tuesday 12